The world we live in

Holly Foulkes

BookLeaf Publishing

India | USA | UK

Presentation by *BookLeaf Publishing*

Web: www.bookleafpub.com

E-mail: info@bookleafpub.com

ISBN : 9789357446952

First edition 2021

DEDICATION

Dedicated to Aaron, Mum, Dad, Tom, Sophie
and Ellie.

PREFACE

These are poems written across one month.
More often than not something would happen or
I would see something that would spark an idea
to write, whether it be at work or at home. I
would grab my notebook and write down exactly
how I felt at that specific moment.

Detached

We live to work.
We work to live.
Each day more empty than the last.
Phlegmatic, we trudge our tired feet
Towards inevitable futures, unavoidable past.
Dark clouds hanging heavy
Like an odorous, saturated towel.
Artificial happiness suffocating, suffocating

Wellness

You must all practice wellness
What the fuck is that?

It's vital for mental health
Only works if you've wealth

When bored it's something they dabble at.

Adult rating

You're an adult now, they say
No help- you're on your own
Faced with failure everyday
And look how we have grown

We really made ourselves something
In a world very different to this
You are only a young little thing
Aged just twenty six

So get up and get moving
Now try not to be a waste
Our bank balance is ever improving
Yet you give up with haste

Sexuality, gender, age, ethnicity
Opportunities for you, are there none?
You long for some stability and
In return we offer, shit jobs with low income

So that you can just afford to pay
For one of our many tiny flats
We'll raise the rent without delay
More money for the bureaucrats

Bad Day

Slippery food molesting skin in the wash basin

Holes in socks making toes feel like turtles with shells too tight

Intermittent wifi connection, bubbling rage

Three times a day we allow these things to upset, and I admit they are horrendous, but every so often, do you turn to pay attention to the infinite beauty and peaceful aura the world so kindly upholds, in our inveterate lives, it has the key to healing, so turn, and behold.

Archie

Archie's majestic
He encapsulates my world
And smells really bad.

I am Happy

I'm trying to be more cheerful
I feel positively upbeat
No, really. The email you just sent?
Hasn't annoyed me, I am complete

Your sly attempts to ruin my day
And drag me to the floor
They wont upset me, oh no
Because I'm not angry anymore.

The internet said to be happy
You need to find a release
This will make you feel engulfed
By a warm and nurturing fleece

Some try yoga, knitting or sports
But when when this simply just wont do
Take yourself to a vast, quiet field. Breathe in
And scream fuck you

You'll feel better.

Kite

Dreaming of distant days
Getting lost in the eye of the comforting wind
It brushes my skin as soft as a feather
Floating through an idyllic, unburdened
existence
So I drift with it
Stepping up into the zephyr
Finally feeling intense release, affirmed
Peace seeps its way into my being
Dreaming of distant days
Getting lost in the eye of the comforting wind

Climate anxiety

I often get this notion
It happens at the end of the day
When in bed-like a curse of potion
That just won't go away

I regress, I'm a vulnerable, scared child
And there's a monster under my bed
My thoughts I attempt to beguile
But they only get stronger instead

Aloud, my thoughts I begin to hear
When it will end I do not know
At night all I have is the vivid idea
That one day the Earth will blow.

Today and all days

Darkness descends heavy as a theatre curtain
Where is the hope?
It is in my soul I am certain
What's the point in the future?
The world has become humanoid
Why do we just cope?

Avoidant, selfish, paranoid
It's self-pity in which we all soak

You

Everyday

I stumble through life
Not knowing where I fit
Ever falling
Ever wondering
Is this really it?

Then I feel you surround me

Soothing like a fresh, warm towel
You whisper our language into my soul
Ever tending
Every doting
It's you that makes me whole

Everyday

Progress

You must hear your heart
For it knows your destiny
Heed the words it sings.

To love

This heart I have- it bulges and sings
To ponder, is it a blessing or curse?
Some declare makes one feel worse
But still- hear how it rings

To love your neighbour is to love yourself
If only all believed this
How the world would be bliss
An experience of serene wealth

Artificial

The world it rolls come what may
The sun it sets and rises
Without care for your worries and woes
You plaster on jovial disguises

You alright?
Yeah, good thanks you?
You long to speak the honest truth
No, please tell me there's something I can do

This earth is made for happiness not
We trudge, we drag, we slog
Endless seems the dreadful hardship
No escape from this filthy bog.

Amber

The sun rests gently on evergreens
Crisp chill of impending Autumn mornings
A calm breeze motioning branches
Summer has turned it's back.

2021

The future is bleak
All hope washed away
My mind becomes weak
Needing to find my way.

A world built for the rich
Inherited, self-made or luck
The poor watch on from their sodden ditch
In poverty and privation we are stuck.

XX

We are the foundation of society
We are emotional glue for all
We are carer's with careers
We are strength
We are unsung
We are women.

Society

Inequality pulses through the bloodstream of our community
Aggressive leeches clinging to conservatism
Someone must be the inferior
For most this fate is chosen at birth
The hierarchy as strong as steel
Those at the bottom desperately climbing the ladder
Those comfortable at the top willing them on
Until they get too close
Peeling a finger off, one at a time- and push
The clamber starts again.

21st century mind

Cascading in a downward spiral
I feel myself slipping
But this is not fiction
There is no Wonderland waiting at the bottom
Just an arduous wait for death

Seek mental health support
21st century's answer to all
Does this heal…
Or simply pull a falsified mask over the pain of
being alive?

A noble profession

Being a teacher
Endless deadlines and data
What about the kids?

Fantasy

Sometimes I dare to dream
Of society being ripped at the seam
The rat race comes to an immediate halt
Removed is it's integral bolt
Poverty obliterated by a beam

So engrained is this vicious life
Stuck in our bones, a malicious knife
This unattainable fantasy
Where humans can just be
Is why we cling to believe there's afterlife.

www.ingramcontent.com/pod-product-compliance
Lightning Source LLC
LaVergne TN
LVHW051251200726
843510LV00011B/1801